EASY AND FUN
KATAKANA

How to Read Non-Japanese Loanwords

Author : Kiyomi Ogawa
English Editor : Orrin Cummins

IBC Publishing

Preface

Some Japanese learners do not place a high importance on learning katakana characters. To be honest, even as a teacher of the language I didn't fully appreciate their value at first. But when I began to observe my surroundings with a more critical eye, I noticed the incredible number of katakana terms in use. It is not an exaggeration to say that practically every word on many restaurant and café menus is written in katakana.

Originally, katakana was used only for *gairaigo*—words imported into the language from other countries—but it is now heavily used in magazines and advertisements due to its inherent "cool factor." Since katakana is used mostly for nouns, understanding it can help you grasp the general idea of a sentence even if you can't fully decipher the grammar. And compared to kanji, katakana characters are much easier to write.

The issue that most foreigners have with katakana has to do with pronunciation. Although most katakana words have their origins in other languages, the way they are pronounced in Japanese is usually quite different. This is partly because the Japanese language is relatively flat, without much rising or falling intonation. So don't get discouraged if it takes you a few seconds to understand a freshly encountered katakana word! The problem is exacerbated by the sizable number of katakana words whose meanings have drifted away from those they held in their original languages.

In this book, I have included many illustrations so that you can know the meanings of words at a glance and get a visual sense of how katakana is used in everyday Japanese life. You will also become familiar with a number of popular *wasei-eigo* terms, some of which seem like English words but won't be recognized as such in English-speaking countries.

Mastering katakana will make reading Japanese more enjoyable!

Kiyomi Ogawa

カバーデザイン：岩目地英樹（コムデザイン）

まえがき

　日本語学習者のなかには、カタカナはひらがなや漢字ほど重要ではないと考えている人がいるようです。実は、私自身も教える立場としてあまり重要視していませんでした。しかし、あたりを見渡してみれば、カタカナ言葉の多いこと！ 特にレストランやカフェのメニューはほとんど全部カタカナといっても過言ではありません。

　カタカナはもともと外来語だけのために使われていましたが、今ではかっこいいからという理由で、雑誌や広告などで多く使われています。さらに、ひらがなは助詞や動詞の一部であるのに対して、カタカナは名詞に使うため、カタカナが読めれば文法がわからなくても意味を理解することができるという利点もあります。書き方も漢字に比べればとてもシンプルで書きやすいでしょう。

　問題は、発音が本来のものとはかなり違って聞こえるということです。日本語はとても平たんな音で、上がり下がりがあまりありません。ですから、カタカナが読めても、一体何のことか理解するのに時間がかかるかもしれません。また元の英語の意味とは違った意味で使われることもありますので、注意しなければなりません。

　本書では、一目見てすぐに意味が分かるように、たくさんのイラストを使用し、カタカナがどんな風に日本の生活に使われているかを視覚的に学ぶことができるように工夫しました。また、日本人がよく使う和製英語も学ぶことができます。

　カタカナをマスターすれば、色々な物を読むのが楽しくなりますよ！

小川清美

How to Use this Book

First, learn how to read and write katakana by working your way through chapter 2.

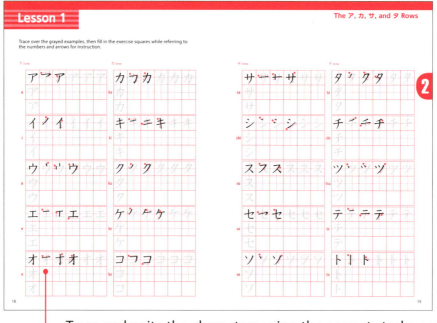

Trace and write the characters using the correct stroke order.

Chapter 3 focuses on how katakana words are used in everyday Japanese life.

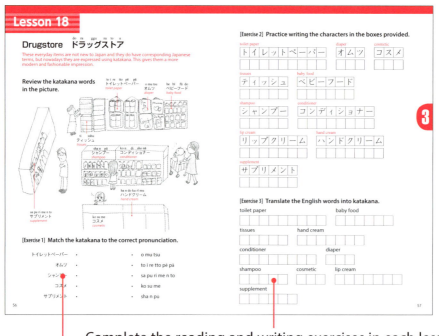

Complete the reading and writing exercises in each lesson.

In chapter 4 you can build your reading skills while learning katakana terms related to people, countries, and business.

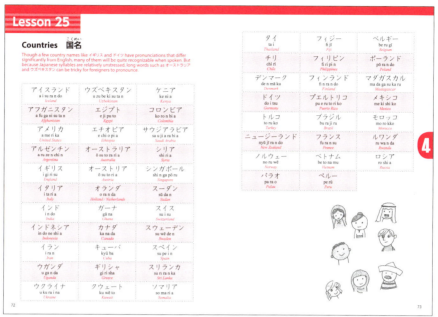

Finally, chapter 5 introduces *wasei-eigo* terms. These are very useful for understanding native Japanese speakers.

Even if you don't have time to complete the writing exercises, I recommend that you at least read chapters 2 and 3 since they contain many indispensable terms for conversing in Japanese.

CONTENTS

Preface   2
How to Use This Book   4

Chapter 1 History and Usage ⑨
第1章　カタカナの歴史と使われ方

History of Katakana　カタカナの歴史　　　　　　　　10
Using Katakana　カタカナの使われ方　　　　　　　　12
Characters and Pronunciation　　　　　　　　　　　14

Chapter 2 Examples and Practice ⑰
第2章　カタカナを書く

Lesson 1　The ア, カ, サ, and タ Rows　　　　　　18
Lesson 2　The ナ, ハ, マ, and ヤ Rows　　　　　　20
Lesson 3　The ラ, ワ, ガ, and ザ Rows　　　　　　22
Lesson 4　The ダ, バ, and パ Rows　　　　　　　　24
Lesson 5　Prolonged Sound Mark　　　　　　　　　26
Lesson 6　Small Characters　　　　　　　　　　　28
Tricky Characters　にている文字　　　　　　　　　30

Chapter 3 Katakana Words ㉝
第3章　カタカナの言葉

Lesson 7　Café Drink Menu　カフェ ドリンク メニュー　34
Lesson 8　Café Menu　カフェ メニュー　　　　　　　36
Lesson 9　Restaurant Menu　レストラン メニュー　　38
Lesson 10　Alcohol　お酒　　　　　　　　　　　　　40

Lesson 11	Fruits and Vegetables　フルーツと野菜	42
Lesson 12	Ramen Shop　ラーメン屋	44
Lesson 13	Foods　食べもの	46
Lesson 14	Kitchen　キッチン	48
Lesson 15	(Bed)room　部屋	50
Lesson 16	Living Room　リビング	52
Lesson 17	Convenience Store　コンビニ	54
Lesson 18	Drugstore　ドラッグストア	56
Lesson 19	Fashion　ファッション	58
Lesson 20	Sports　スポーツ	60
Lesson 21	Automobiles　車	62
Lesson 22	Around Town　町の中	64
Lesson 23	Advertisements　広告	66
Lesson 24	Instruments　楽器	68

Chapter 4　People, Places, and Business　71
第4章　人・場所・ビジネスに関するカタカナ

Lesson 25	Countries　国名	72
Lesson 26	English Names　英語名	74
Lesson 27	Companies　会社名	76
Lesson 28	Business Terms　ビジネス用語	78
Lesson 29	Computer Terms　コンピューター用語	80

Chapter 5　*Wasei-Eigo* and Other Terms　83
第5章　和製英語など

Lesson 30	*Wasei-Eigo* 1　和製英語1	84
Lesson 31	*Wasei-Eigo* 2　和製英語2	86
Lesson 32	Other Terms　その他	88

Chapter 1
History and Usage

第 1 章　カタカナの歴史と使われ方

History of Katakana

It is said that katakana was originally developed around the eighth century for reading Buddhist sutras transmitted from China. To aid in reciting the texts, monks created a sort of shorthand by simplifying the Chinese characters. Other theories exist, but this is the most generally accepted one.

In contrast to hiragana characters, each of which represents a simplified version of an entire kanji, the katakana characters were created by taking only a portion of the corresponding kanji.

Kanji		Katakana	Kanji		Hiragana
伊	→	イ	以	→	い
呂	→	ロ	呂	→	ろ

The monks added these modified characters next to the kanji as a pronunciation guide. Although the katakana script started out as a simple note-taking method for Buddhist monks and intellectuals, starting in the Meiji era it gained popularity among common citizens as a way to express foreign words (*gairaigo*). During this period, women even used katakana to write their names.

Katakana is currently taught after hiragana at elementary schools in Japan.

カタカナの歴史

　カタカナは8世紀ごろ中国から仏教が伝わった時に、仏教の経典を書き写すために作られたと言われています。僧侶たちが漢字の一部を簡素化したのです。他の説もありますが、これがいまのところ有力なようです。

　ひらがなは漢字全体を簡素化していますが、カタカナは漢字の一部だけを取って簡素化しています。

漢字		カタカナ	漢字		ひらがな
伊	→	イ	以	→	い
呂	→	ロ	呂	→	ろ

　このように簡単にしたものを僧侶たちは漢字の横につけて読んでいました。ですから、もともとは僧侶や知識人が漢字を読む際の注記として使っていましたが、明治以降に外来語に使われるようになり、一般の人々にも使われるようになったようです。またその頃、女性の名前にも多く使われました。

　現在は小学校でひらがなの次に学ばれています。

Using Katakana

Katakana is used for *gairago*, or words from other languages which have been adopted into Japanese. This of course includes the names of foreign countries and people, but also a great many other terms related to food, technology, and miscellaneous products. Although katakana words are based on these foreign counterparts, their pronunciations can differ significantly from the original words, making them surprisingly tricky for foreigners.

And even in cases where a Japanese word already exists for a particular concept, *gairaigo* is often used in magazines and advertisements because it sounds stylish to Japanese people. Among these are a number of words whose meanings or usages differ from those found in the source languages. Such terms are known as *wasei-eigo*, or "Japanese English."

The katakana script also has a certain stylistic effect from a visual standpoint. Compared to hiragana or kanji, katakana creates a casual or comical impression; this is why colloquial expressions and onomatopoeia are often written in katakana. Katakana is widely used for company and product names for the same reason.

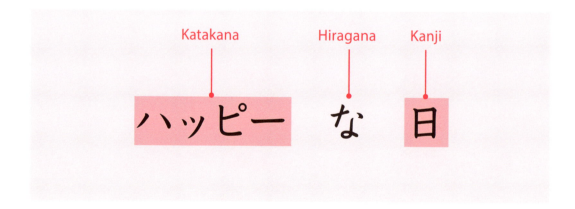

カタカナの使われ方

　カタカナは主に外来語つまり外国から来た言葉に使います。国の名前や人名をはじめ、食べ物、雑貨、IT用語などに多く使われています。しかし、発音は本来の外国語とはかなり違って聞こえるので外国人には難しいようです。

　また、外来語で本来の日本語表記がある場合でも、外国語のほうが日本人にはおしゃれに聞こえるので、雑誌や広告ではカタカナを用いることが多いようです。中には外国語の本来の意味から外れている言葉もあり、それらを和製英語と呼んでいます。

　カタカナには視覚的な効果もあります。ひらがなや漢字と比べて、カタカナは軽くておもしろい印象があるので、くだけた表現やオノマトペをカタカナで表すことが多くあります。同様の理由で会社名や商品名にも使用されています。

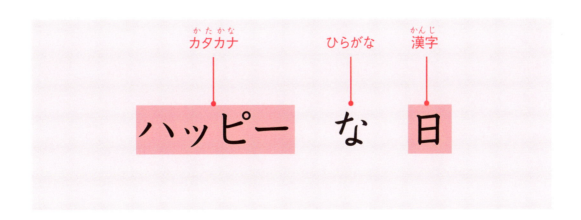

Characters and Pronunciation

This syllable set is primarily used for words borrowed from other languages, but it is also widely adopted into logos, slang speech, and other formats.

Katakana

Basic syllables

a ア	i イ	u ウ	e エ	o オ
ka カ	ki キ	ku ク	ke ケ	ko コ
sa サ	shi シ	su ス	se セ	so ソ
ta タ	chi チ	tsu ツ	te テ	to ト
na ナ	ni ニ	nu ヌ	ne ネ	no ノ
ha/wa ハ	hi ヒ	fu フ	he/e ヘ	ho ホ
ma マ	mi ミ	mu ム	me メ	mo モ
ya ヤ		yu ユ		yo ヨ
ra ラ	ri リ	ru ル	re レ	ro ロ
wa ワ				wo/o ヲ
n ン				

kya キャ	kyu キュ	kyo キョ	
sha シャ	shu シュ	sho ショ	
cha チャ	chu チュ	cho チョ	
nya ニャ	nyu ニュ	nyo ニョ	
hya ヒャ	hyu ヒュ	hyo ヒョ	
mya ミャ	myu ミュ	myo ミョ	
rya リャ	ryu リュ	ryo リョ	

Modified syllables

ga ガ	gi ギ	gu グ	ge ゲ	go ゴ
za ザ	ji ジ	zu ズ	ze ゼ	zo ゾ
da ダ	ji ヂ	zu ヅ	de デ	do ド
ba バ	bi ビ	bu ブ	be ベ	bo ボ
pa パ	pi ピ	pu プ	pe ペ	po ポ

gya ギャ	gyu ギュ	gyo ギョ	
ja ジャ	ju ジュ	jo ジョ	
bya ビャ	byu ビュ	byo ビョ	
pya ピャ	pyu ピュ	pyo ピョ	

The hiragana syllabary contains 46 basic characters. Five of these represent syllables (あ, い, う, え, お) which are phonetically combined with consonants to form the remaining characters. In addition, many characters can be modified using the accent marks 「゛」 or 「゜」 to form slightly different sounds. Variants created by appending a small ゃ, ゅ, or ょ also exist.

Hiragana

Basic syllables

a	あ	i	い	u	う	e	え	o	お
ka	か	ki	き	ku	く	ke	け	ko	こ
sa	さ	shi	し	su	す	se	せ	so	そ
ta	た	chi	ち	tsu	つ	te	て	to	と
na	な	ni	に	nu	ぬ	ne	ね	no	の
ha/wa	は	hi	ひ	fu	ふ	he/e	へ	ho	ほ
ma	ま	mi	み	mu	む	me	め	mo	も
ya	や			yu	ゆ			yo	よ
ra	ら	ri	り	ru	る	re	れ	ro	ろ
wa	わ							wo/o	を
n	ん								

kya	きゃ	kyu	きゅ	kyo	きょ
sha	しゃ	shu	しゅ	sho	しょ
cha	ちゃ	chu	ちゅ	cho	ちょ
nya	にゃ	nyu	にゅ	nyo	にょ
hya	ひゃ	hyu	ひゅ	hyo	ひょ
mya	みゃ	myu	みゅ	myo	みょ

rya	りゃ	ryu	りゅ	ryo	りょ

Modified syllables

ga	が	gi	ぎ	gu	ぐ	ge	げ	go	ご
za	ざ	ji	じ	zu	ず	ze	ぜ	zo	ぞ
da	だ	ji	ぢ	zu	づ	de	で	do	ど
ba	ば	bi	び	bu	ぶ	be	べ	bo	ぼ
pa	ぱ	pi	ぴ	pu	ぷ	pe	ぺ	po	ぽ

gya	ぎゃ	gyu	ぎゅ	gyo	ぎょ
ja	じゃ	ju	じゅ	jo	じょ

bya	びゃ	byu	びゅ	byo	びょ
pya	ぴゃ	pyu	ぴゅ	pyo	ぴょ

Chapter 2

Examples and Practice

第2章　カタカナを書く

Lesson 1

Trace over the grayed examples, then fill in the exercise squares while referring to the numbers and arrows for instruction.

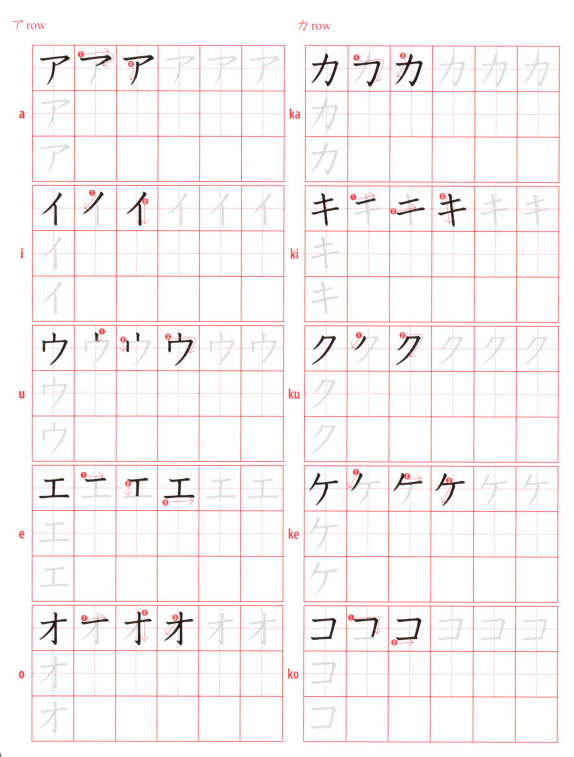

18

The ア, カ, サ, and タ Rows

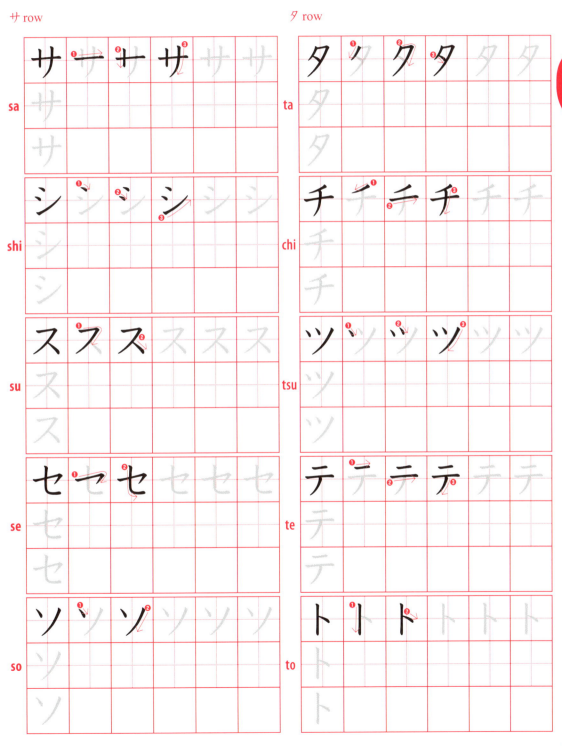

Lesson 2

Trace over the grayed examples, then fill in the exercise squares while referring to the numbers and arrows for instruction.

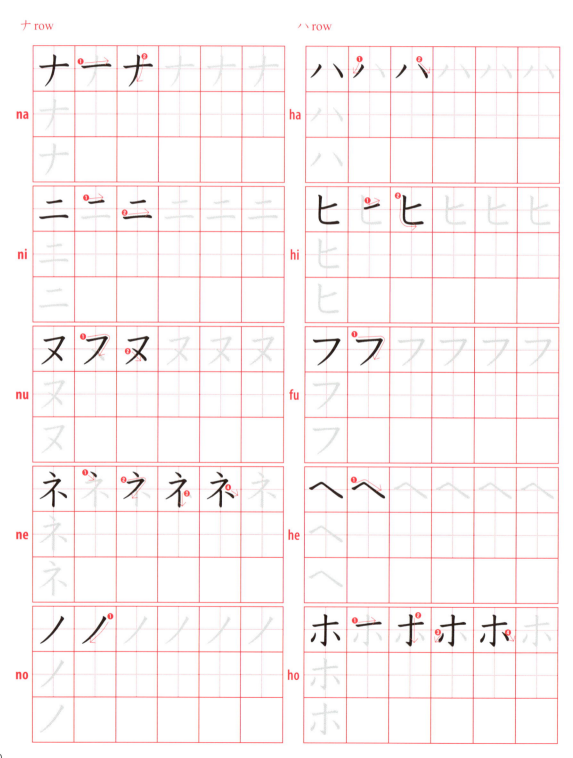

The ナ, ハ, マ, and ヤ Rows

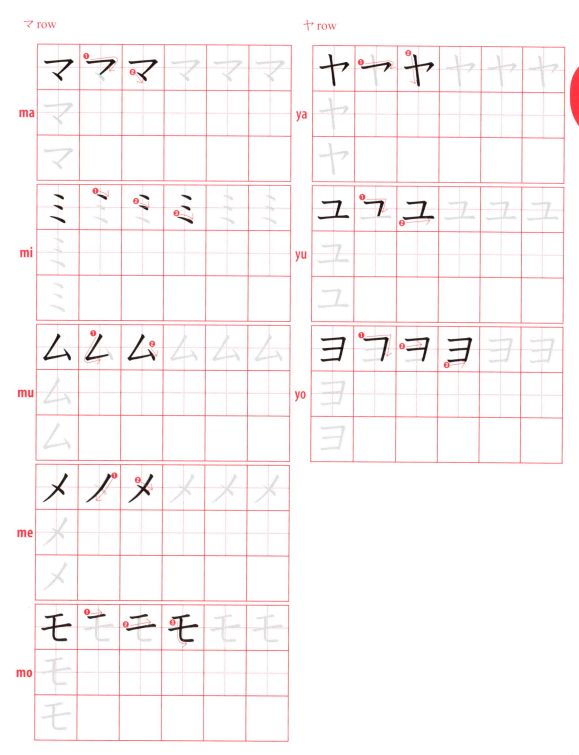

Lesson 3

Trace over the grayed examples, then fill in the exercise squares while referring to the numbers and arrows for instruction.

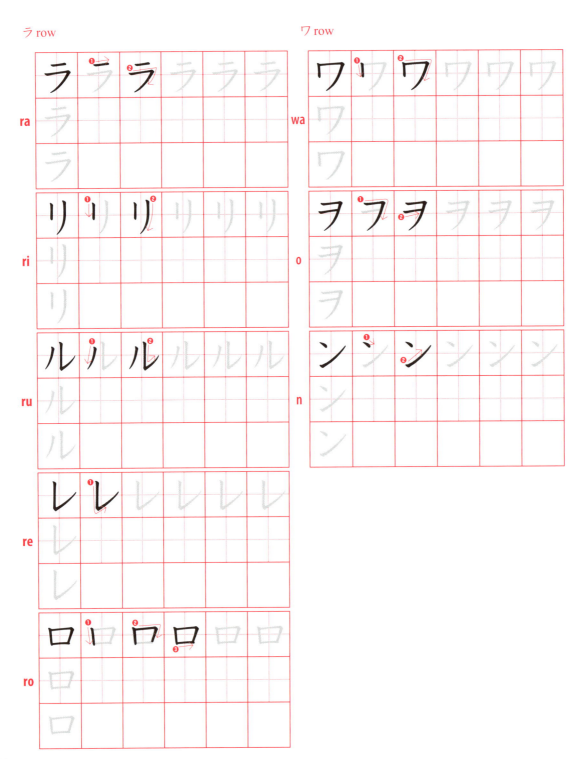

The ラ, ワ, ガ, and ザ Rows

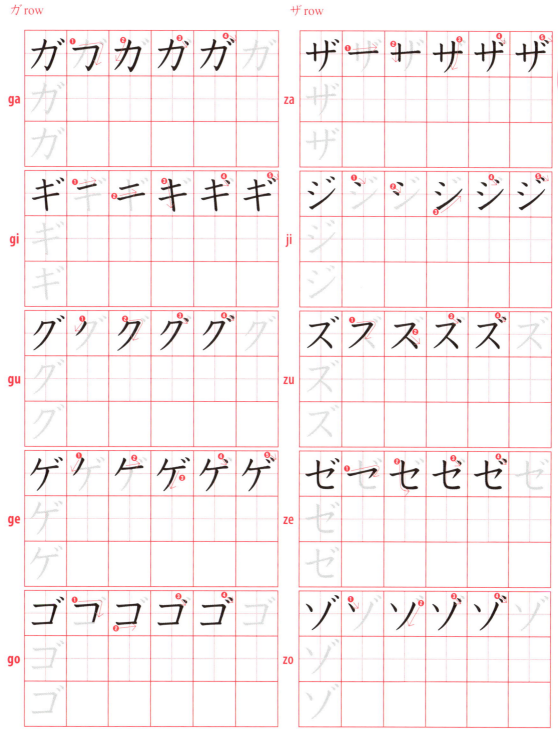

Lesson 4

Trace over the grayed examples, then fill in the exercise squares while referring to the numbers and arrows for instruction.

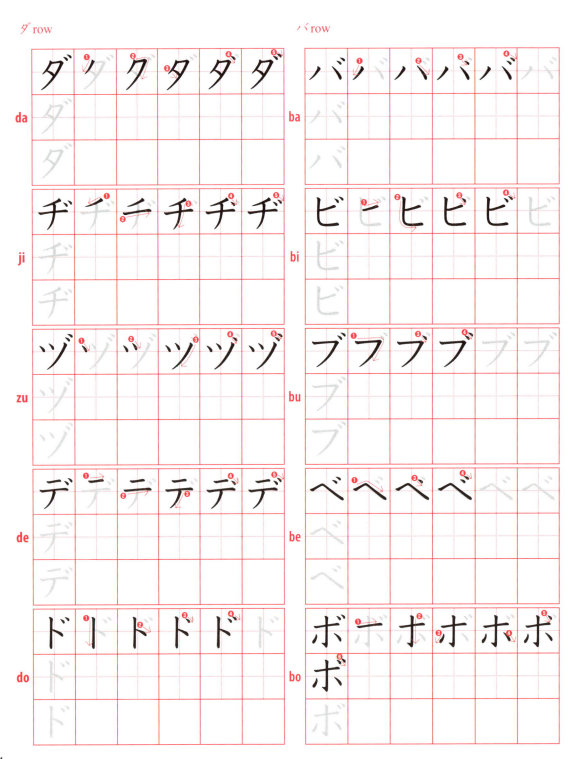

The ダ, バ, and パ Rows

パ row

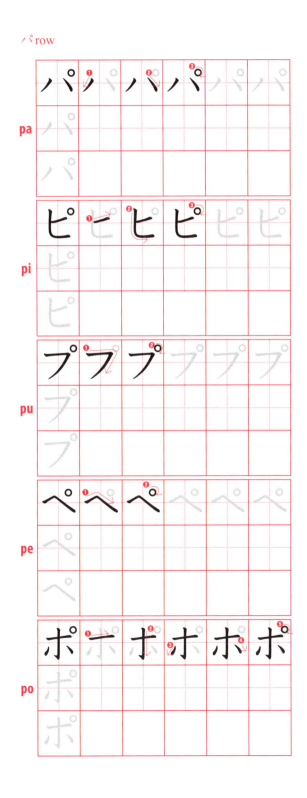

pa

pi

pu

pe

po

Lesson 5

Since the Japanese language does not contain a soft [r] sound, words such as the following are written using the prolonged sound mark.

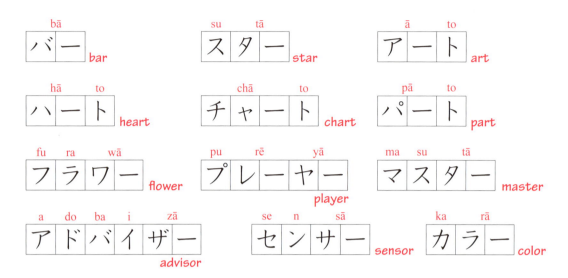

This long mark is also used for the following words.

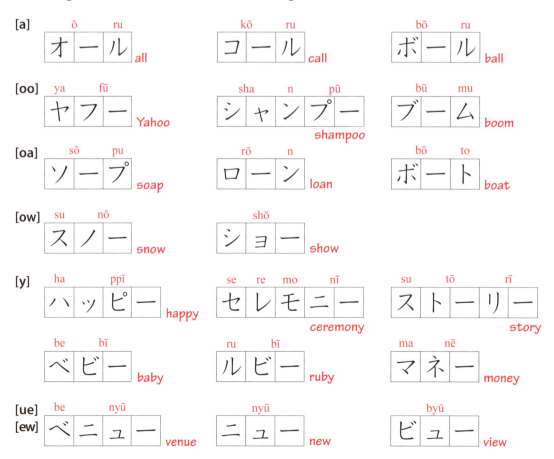

Prolonged Sound Mark

A   Translate the English words into katakana.

1   art

2   part

3   flower

4   boat

5   sensor

6   Yahoo

B   Match the following katakana words to their English counter parts.

オール　•　　　　　•　snow

ブーム　•　　　　　•　ceremony

スノー　•　　　　　•　all

ベビー　•　　　　　•　baby

セレモニー　•　　　•　boom

Lesson 6

The small [tsu] (ッ) isn't pronounced—it merely indicates a slight pause before the pronunciation of the following syllable.

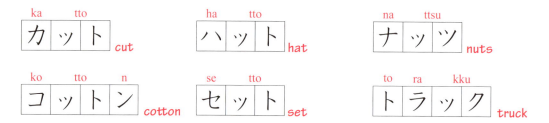

Small vowels (ァ, ィ, ゥ, ェ, ォ) and small "Y" characters (ャ, ュ, ョ) modify the pronunciation of the preceding character by replacing its vowel sound. This allows for the creation of some sounds which are not originally found in Japanese. For example, there is no kana character for approximating the [fi] sound in the English word "fish." But by combining フ with a small ィ, we can replace the [u] vowel sound on the end of フ with the ィ sound (which in Japanese is pronounced like a long [ee] in English).

small アイウエオ

small ヤユヨ

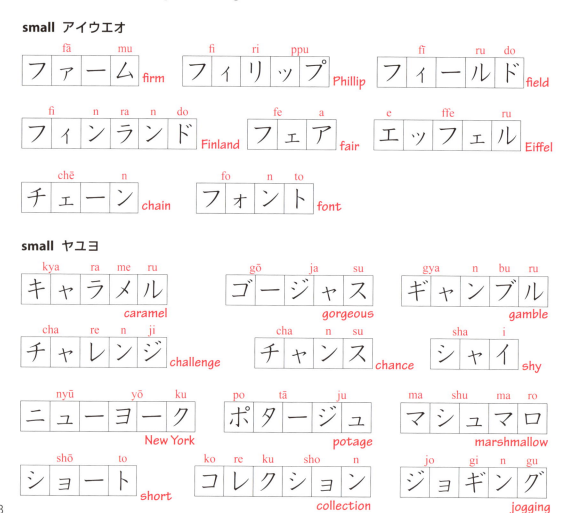

Small Characters

A Write the following English words in katakana.

1 hat □□□

2 truck □□□□

3 font □□□□

4 shy □□□

5 gamble □□□□□

6 marshmallow □□□□□

B Match each katakana word to its English equivalent.

コットン • • caramel

フィールド • • cotton

キャラメル • • collection

チャンス • • chance

コレクション • • field

Tricky Characters

These characters have similar shapes, so take extra care when using them.

にている文字

Which one is correct?

1 a i su
  a アイス
  b マイス

2 shī tsu
  a ツーシ
  b シーツ

3 pa n da
  a パソダ
  b パンダ

4 sū pu
  a スープ
  b ヌープ

5 ko a ra
  a コアラ
  b ユアラ

6 me ro n
  a ナロン
  b メロン

7 te ni su
  a チニス
  b テニス

8 wa i n
  a ワイン
  b ウイン

Answer : *English*

1 a / *ice cream*   4 a / *soup*   7 b / *tennis*
2 b / *sheets*   5 a / *koala*   8 a / *wine*
3 b / *panda*   6 b / *melon*

31

Chapter 3

Katakana Words

第3章　カタカナの言葉

Lesson 7

Café Drink Menu カフェ ドリンクメニュー
<small>ka fe do ri n ku me nyū</small>

Since many items found on café menus are direct cultural imports to Japan, you will probably recognize most of them.

Review the katakana words in the picture.

ka fe o re
カフェオレ
café au lait

ka fe ra te
カフェラテ
caffé latte

koko a
ココア
cocoa

a me ri ka n kō hī
アメリカンコーヒー
American coffee

e su pu re sso
エスプレッソ
espresso

ho tto mi ru ku tī
ホットミルクティー
tea with milk

ho tto re mo n tī
ホットレモンティー
tea with lemon

bu re n do kō hī
ブレンドコーヒー
blended coffee

a i su ka fe o re
アイスカフェオレ
iced café au lait

a i su ka fe ra te
アイスカフェラテ
iced caffé latte

kō ra
コーラ
cola

a i su kō hī
アイスコーヒー
iced coffee

kō hī fu rō to
コーヒーフロート
coffee float

o re n ji jū su
オレンジジュース
orange juice

[Exercise 1] Match the katakana to the correct pronunciation.

- ブレンドコーヒー •   • e su pu re sso
- エスプレッソ •   • bu re n do kō hī
- ココア •   • o re n ji jū su
- コーヒーフロート •   • kō hī fu rō to
- オレンジジュース •   • ko ko a

[Exercise 2] Practice writing the characters in the boxes provided.

[Exercise 3] Translate the English words into katakana.

blended coffee

tea with milk

espresso

iced coffee

cocoa

café au lait

cola

orange juice

American coffee

coffee float

tea with lemon

caffé latte

Lesson 8

Café Menu カフェ メニュー
ka fe　me nyū

Cafés that serve Western food are very popular in Japan.

Review the katakana words in the picture.

[Exercise 1] Match the katakana to the correct pronunciation.

ロールケーキ　•　　　　•　dō na tsu

アップルパイ　•　　　　•　ku ro wa ssa n

クロワッサン　•　　　　•　rō ru kē ki

ドーナツ　　•　　　　•　a ppu ru pa i

パフェ　　　•　　　　•　pa fe

[Exercise 2] Practice writing the characters in the boxes provided.

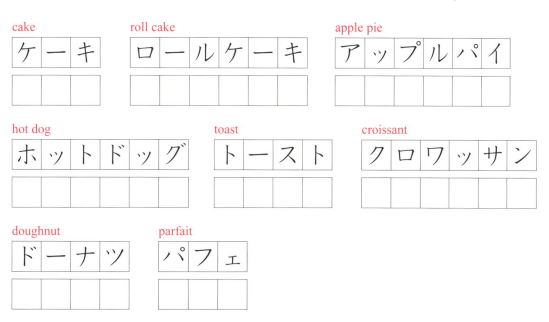

[Exercise 3] Translate the English words into katakana.

roll cake

apple pie

hot dog

toast

croissant

doughnut

parfait

Lesson 9

Restaurant Menu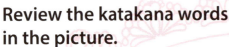
re su to ra n   me nyū
レストラン メニュー

Places that serve *wa-shoku* (traditional Japanese cuisine) will generally have menus written in kanji, but there are also many Western-style restaurants where the menus will appear largely in katakana.

Review the katakana words in the picture.

[Exercise 1] Match the katakana to the correct pronunciation.

パスタ　　•　　　　　　　•　ha n bā gu

ハンバーグ　•　　　　　　　•　o mu ra i su

ステーキ　　•　　　　　　　•　pa su ta

オムライス　•　　　　　　　•　ka rē ra i su

カレーライス　•　　　　　　•　su tē ki

[Exercise 2] Practice writing the characters in the boxes provided.

pasta
パ	ス	タ

spaghetti
ス	パ	ゲ	ッ	テ	ィ

Salisbury steak
ハ	ン	バ	ー	グ

pizza
ピ	ザ

steak
ス	テ	ー	キ

lunch set
ラ	ン	チ	セ	ッ	ト

omelet on rice
オ	ム	ラ	イ	ス

curry rice
カ	レ	ー	ラ	イ	ス

[Exercise 3] Translate the English words into katakana.

pasta

spaghetti

Salisbury steak

pizza

steak

lunch set

omelet on rice

curry rice

Lesson 10

Alcohol お酒(さけ)

Japan has some unique variations on alcoholic drinks. One popular item is a mixture of Japanese liquor and flavored soda water known as a チューハイ or "shōchū highball."

Review the katakana words in the picture.

[Exercise 1] Match the katakana to the correct pronunciation.

ビール　・　　　　　・　u i su kī

ワイン　・　　　　　・　ka ku te ru

カクテル　・　　　　　・　wa i n

ウイスキー　・　　　　　・　bī ru

チューハイ　・　　　　　・　chū ha i

[Exercise 2] Practice writing the characters in the boxes provided.

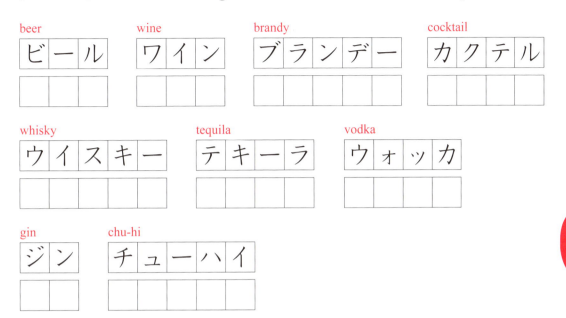

[Exercise 3] Translate the English words into katakana.

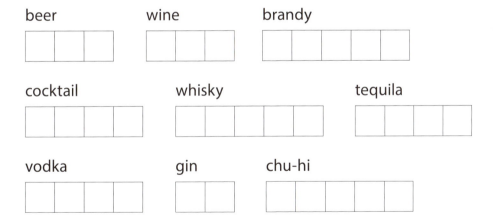

Lesson 11

Fruits and Vegetables フルーツと野菜
(fu rū tsu) (ya sai)

These terms will be fairly obvious to an English native speaker, with a few notable exceptions: ピーマン is derived from the French word for green bell pepper (piment), and サニーレタス refers to a type of red-leaf lettuce commonly sold in Japan.

Review the katakana words in the picture.

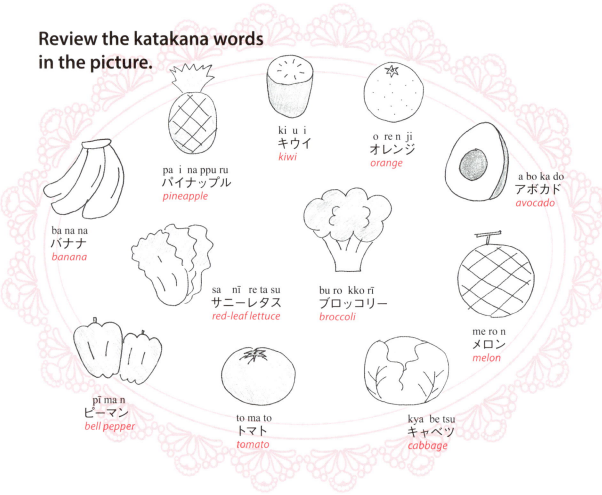

ki u i キウイ *kiwi*
o re n ji オレンジ *orange*
pa i na ppu ru パイナップル *pineapple*
a bo ka do アボカド *avocado*
ba na na バナナ *banana*
sa nī re ta su サニーレタス *red-leaf lettuce*
bu ro kko rī ブロッコリー *broccoli*
me ro n メロン *melon*
pī ma n ピーマン *bell pepper*
to ma to トマト *tomato*
kya be tsu キャベツ *cabbage*

[Exercise 1] Match the katakana to the correct pronunciation.

バナナ •   • ba na na

オレンジ •   • to ma to

サニーレタス •   • o re n ji

トマト •   • kya be tsu

キャベツ •   • sa nī re ta su

[Exercise 2] Practice writing the characters in the boxes provided.

[Exercise 3] Translate the English words into katakana.

banana

pineapple

kiwi

orange

avocado

melon

red-leaf lettuce

bell pepper

broccoli

tomato

cabbage

Lesson 12

Ramen Shop ラーメン屋 (rā me n ya)

Many of these words were imported from Chinese and have corresponding pronunciations. Although each term can also be represented using kanji, katakana is widely used instead because it is easier to read.

Review the katakana words in the picture.

- ネギ (ne gi) — green onion
- シューマイ (shū ma i) — dumpling
- ギョーザ (gyō za) — jiaozi (Chinese dumplings)
- メンマ (me n ma) — boiled bamboo shoots
- チャーシュー (chā shū) — char siu (sliced pork)
- ナルト (na ru to) — naruto
- ラーメン (rā me n) — ramen
- チャーハン (chā ha n) — fried rice
- スープ (sū pu) — soup
- ライス (ra i su) — rice

[Exercise 1] Match the katakana to the correct pronunciation.

チャーハン •	• rā me n
ラーメン •	• chā ha n
ネギ •	• shū ma i
シューマイ •	• ne gi
ライス •	• ra i su

[Exercise 2] **Practice writing the characters in the boxes provided.**

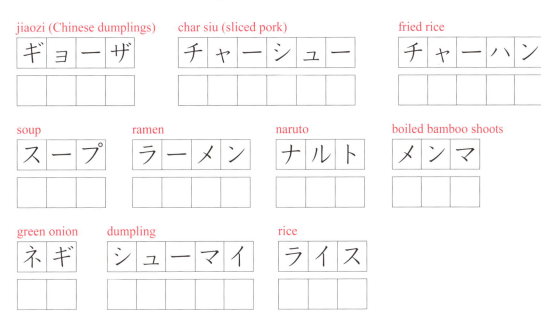

[Exercise 3] **Translate the English words into katakana.**

jiaozi (Chinese dumplings)

char siu (sliced pork)

soup

ramen

naruto

green onion

dumpling

rice

boiled bamboo shoots

Lesson 13

Foods 食(た)べもの

Since ingredients like チーズ and バター were not traditionally used in Japanese cuisine, there are no kanji to represent them and they aren't written in hiragana. マヨネーズ is very popular in Japan and is often shortened to マヨ.

Review the katakana words in the picture.

ba tā
バター
butter

ja mu
ジャム
jam

chī zu
チーズ
cheese

mā ga ri n
マーガリン
margarine

do re sshi n gu
ドレッシング
salad dressing

ma yo nē zu
マヨネーズ
mayonnaise

ke cha ppu
ケチャップ
ketchup

o rī bu o i ru
オリーブオイル
olive oil

ka rē rū
カレールー
curry roux

[Exercise 1] Match the katakana to the correct pronunciation.

チーズ • • ma yo nē zu

マーガリン • • do re sshi n gu

マヨネーズ • • ka rē rū

ドレッシング • • mā ga ri n

カレールー • • chī zu

46

[Exercise 2] Practice writing the characters in the boxes provided.

cheese
チーズ

butter
バター

jam
ジャム

margarine
マーガリン

ketchup
ケチャップ

mayonnaise
マヨネーズ

salad dressing
ドレッシング

olive oil
オリーブオイル

curry roux
カレールー

[Exercise 3] Translate the English words into katakana.

cheese

butter

jam

margarine

ketchup

mayonnaise

salad dressing

olive oil

curry roux

Lesson 14

Kitchen キッチン
<small>ki tchi n</small>

Terms for describing kitchen appliances are largely imported from other languages, but be careful: some of them are completely different than their English counterparts, such as レンジ and ガステーブル.

Review the katakana words in the picture.

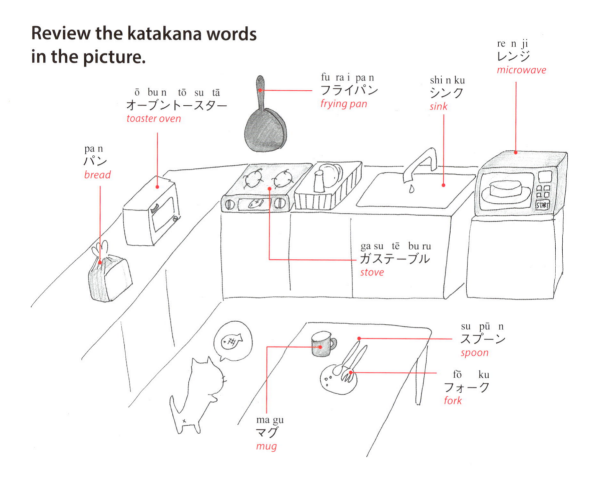

[Exercise 1] Match the katakana to the correct pronunciation.

パン　　　•　　　　　　　•　ga su tē bu ru

フライパン　•　　　　　　•　re n ji

ガステーブル　•　　　　　•　pa n

レンジ　　•　　　　　　　•　fō ku

フォーク　•　　　　　　　•　fu ra i pa n

[Exercise 2] Practice writing the characters in the boxes provided.

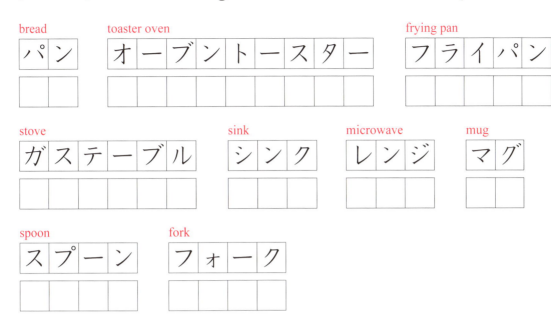

[Exercise 3] Translate the English words into katakana.

bread

toaster oven

frying pan

stove

sink

microwave

mug

spoon

fork

Lesson 15

(Bed)room 部屋(へや)

Almost all of these terms are direct English imports, although the Japanese like to abbreviate them; スマートホン becomes スマホ, パーソナル・コンピューター becomes パソコン, etc.

Review the katakana words in the picture.

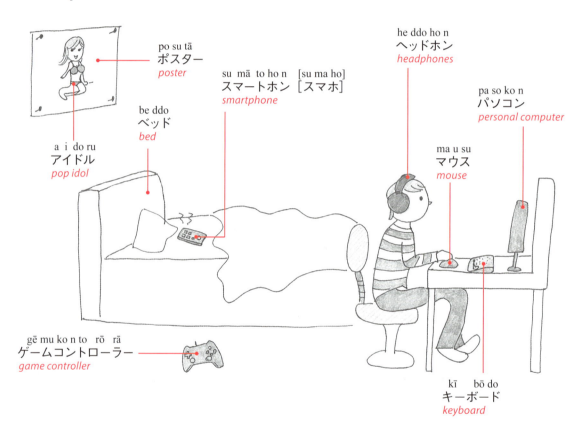

[Exercise 1] Match the katakana to the correct pronunciation.

アイドル　・　　　　　　　　・　a i do ru

ベッド　　・　　　　　　　　・　su mā to ho n

スマートホン　・　　　　　　・　pa so ko n

キーボード　・　　　　　　　・　kī bō do

パソコン　・　　　　　　　　・　be ddo

[Exercise 2] Practice writing the characters in the boxes provided.

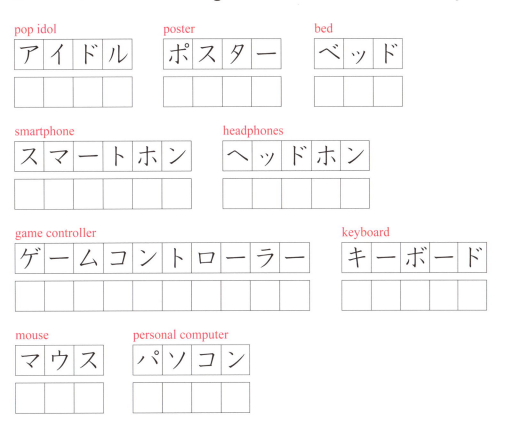

[Exercise 3] Translate the English words into katakana.

pop idol

poster

bed

personal computer

smartphone

game controller

headphones

keyboard

mouse

Lesson 16

Living Room　リビング (ri bi n gu)

Modern Japanese homes have been Westernized to a large extent, and traditional tatami rooms are becoming scarce. As a result, many items found in these rooms are described using imported words.

Review the katakana words in the picture.

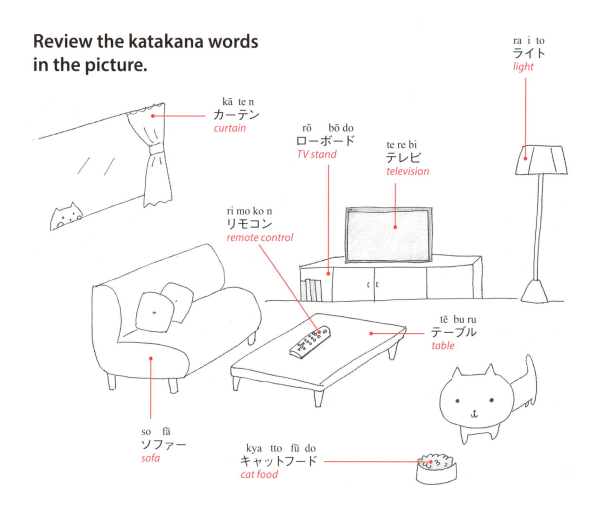

- カーテン (kā te n) — curtain
- ローボード (rō bō do) — TV stand
- テレビ (te re bi) — television
- ライト (ra i to) — light
- リモコン (ri mo ko n) — remote control
- テーブル (tē bu ru) — table
- ソファー (so fā) — sofa
- キャットフード (kya tto fū do) — cat food

[Exercise 1] Match the katakana to the correct pronunciation.

カーテン •	• tē bu ru
テレビ •	• te re bi
リモコン •	• kā te n
テーブル •	• ri mo ko n
ライト •	• ra i to

[Exercise 2] Practice writing the characters in the boxes provided.

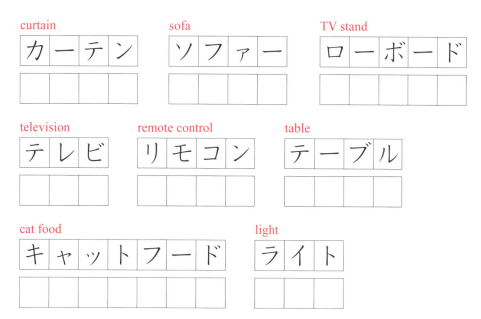

[Exercise 3] Translate the English words into katakana.

curtain

sofa

TV stand

remote control

table

cat food

light

television

Lesson 17

Convenience Store コンビニ
<small>ko n bi ni</small>

Much of the food found in convenience stores is described using terms that will be familiar to English speakers, but take note of the few oddities such as レジ and トイレ. The word コンビニエンス itself is usually shortened to コンビニ.

Review the katakana words in the picture.

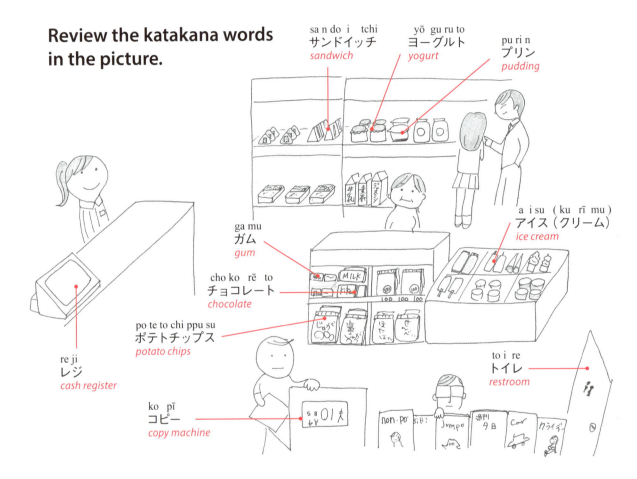

[Exercise 1] **Match the katakana to the correct pronunciation.**

レジ   •   • ga mu

コピー   •   • sa n do i tchi

ガム   •   • ko pī

トイレ   •   • to i re

サンドイッチ •   • re ji

[Exercise 2] Practice writing the characters in the boxes provided.

cash register: レジ

copy machine: コピー

chocolate: チョコレート

gum: ガム

potato chips: ポテトチップス

ice cream: アイスクリーム

rest room: トイレ

sandwich: サンドイッチ

yogurt: ヨーグルト

pudding: プリン

[Exercise 3] Translate the English words into katakana.

cash register

copy machine

chocolate

gum

potato chips

ice cream

sandwich

yogurt

pudding

Lesson 18

Drugstore ドラッグストア
do ra ggu su to a

These everyday items are not new to Japan and they do have corresponding Japanese terms, but nowadays they are expressed using katakana. This gives them a more modern and fashionable impression.

Review the katakana words in the picture.

[Exercise 1] Match the katakana to the correct pronunciation.

トイレットペーパー •	• o mu tsu
オムツ •	• to i re tto pē pā
シャンプー •	• sa pu ri me n to
コスメ •	• ko su me
サプリメント •	• sha n pū

[Exercise 2] Practice writing the characters in the boxes provided.

toilet paper
トイレットペーパー

diaper
オムツ

cosmetic
コスメ

tissues
ティッシュ

baby food
ベビーフード

shampoo
シャンプー

conditioner
コンディショナー

lip cream
リップクリーム

hand cream
ハンドクリーム

supplement
サプリメント

[Exercise 3] Translate the English words into katakana.

toilet paper

baby food

tissues

hand cream

conditioner

diaper

shampoo

cosmetic

lip cream

supplement

Lesson 19

Fashion ファッション
<small>fa ssho n</small>

As traditional Japanese clothing was worn up until the dawn of the Meiji period, these words are all imported from English. Fashion magazines and catalogs almost always use katakana to describe these sorts of items.

Review the katakana words in the picture.

[Exercise 1] **Match the katakana to the correct pronunciation.**

セーター　•　　　　　•　sū tsu

スカート　•　　　　　•　su kā to

ジャケット　•　　　　•　ba ggu

バッグ　•　　　　　　•　ja ke tto

スーツ　•　　　　　　•　sē tā

[Exercise 2] Practice writing the characters in the boxes provided.

sweater	skirt	loafers
セーター	スカート	ローファー

muffler	jacket	bag	suit
マフラー	ジャケット	バッグ	スーツ

handkerchief	high heels	necktie
ハンカチ	ハイヒール	ネクタイ

[Exercise 3] Translate the English words into katakana.

sweater

skirt

loafers

muffler

jacket

high heels

bag

handkerchief

suit

necktie

Lesson 20

Sports スポーツ
su pō tsu

Sports like judo and karate which originated in Japan have their own kanji, but most others are written in katakana. Abbreviations such as バスケ for バスケットボール and バレー for バレーボール are also common.

Review the katakana words in the picture.

ba su ke tto bō ru
バスケットボール
basketball

ba rē bō ru
バレーボール
volleyball

su kī
スキー
skiing

go ru fu
ゴルフ
golf

ra n ni n gu
ランニング
running

te ni su
テニス
tennis

sa kkā
サッカー
soccer

fi gyu a su kē to
フィギュアスケート
figure skating

[Exercise 1] Match the katakana to the correct pronunciation.

バスケットボール • • fi gyu a su kē to

テニス • • go ru fu

サッカー • • sa kkā

フィギュアスケート • • te ni su

ゴルフ • • ba su ke tto bō ru

[Exercise 2] Practice writing the characters in the boxes provided.

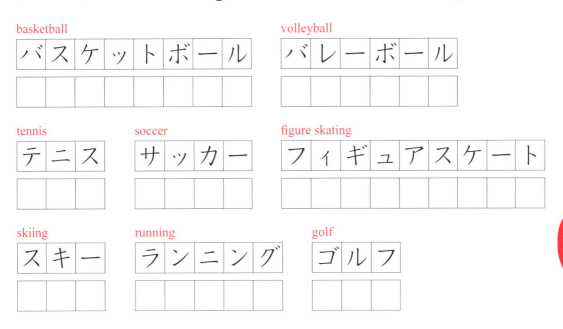

[Exercise 3] Translate the English words into katakana.

basketball

volleyball

tennis

soccer

figure skating

skiing

running

golf

Lesson 21

Automobiles 車(くるま)

Automobile-related terms are all written in katakana, but for some reason they often differ from their English equivalents.

Review the katakana words in the picture.

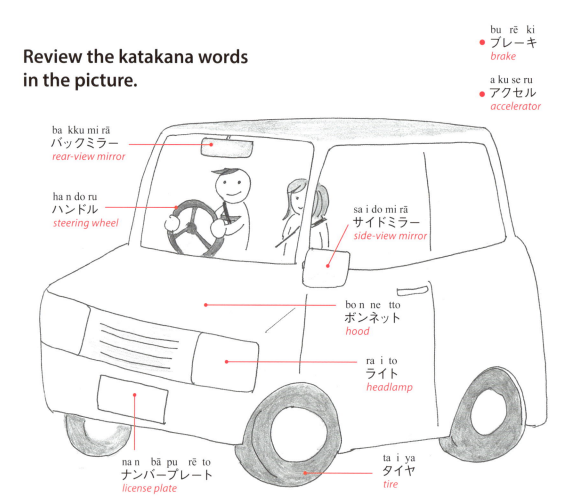

- bu rē ki
  ブレーキ
  brake
- a ku se ru
  アクセル
  accelerator
- ba kku mi rā
  バックミラー
  rear-view mirror
- ha n do ru
  ハンドル
  steering wheel
- sa i do mi rā
  サイドミラー
  side-view mirror
- bo n ne tto
  ボンネット
  hood
- ra i to
  ライト
  headlamp
- na n bā pu rē to
  ナンバープレート
  license plate
- ta i ya
  タイヤ
  tire

[Exercise 1] Match the katakana to the correct pronunciation.

ハンドル   •   •   na n bā pu rē to

バックミラー   •   •   a ku se ru

ナンバープレート •   •   bu rē ki

ブレーキ   •   •   ha n do ru

アクセル   •   •   ba kku mi rā

[Exercise 2] Practice writing the characters in the boxes provided.

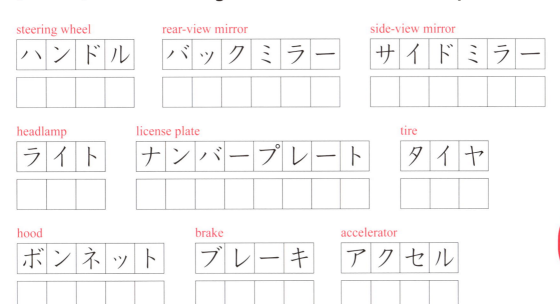

[Exercise 3] Translate the English words into katakana.

steering wheel

rear-view mirror

side-view mirror

headlamp

license plate

tire

hood

brake

accelerator

Lesson 22

Around Town 町_{まち}の中_{なか}

Though ビジネスホテル were originally created for company employees on business trips, they have become popular among normal travelers as well due to their low cost and convenience.

Review the katakana words in the picture.

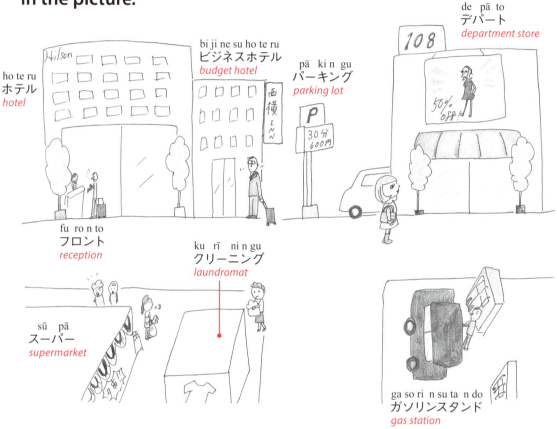

ho te ru
ホテル
hotel

bi ji ne su ho te ru
ビジネスホテル
budget hotel

pā ki n gu
パーキング
parking lot

de pā to
デパート
department store

fu ro n to
フロント
reception

ku rī ni n gu
クリーニング
laundromat

sū pā
スーパー
supermarket

ga so ri n su ta n do
ガソリンスタンド
gas station

[Exercise 1] Match the katakana to the correct pronunciation.

ビジネスホテル　・　　　　・　ga so ri n su ta n do

フロント　・　　　　・　fu ro n to

ガソリンスタンド　・　　　　・　de pā to

スーパー　・　　　　・　bi ji ne su ho te ru

デパート　・　　　　・　sū pā

[Exercise 2] Practice writing the characters in the boxes provided.

hotel
ホテル

budget hotel
ビジネスホテル

reception
フロント

gas station
ガソリンスタンド

laundromat
クリーニング

supermarket
スーパー

department store
デパート

parking lot
パーキング

[Exercise 3] Translate the English words into katakana.

hotel

budget hotel

reception

gas station

laundromat

supermarket

department store

parking lot

Lesson 23

Advertisements 広告(こうこく)

Katakana is widely used in advertisements because it gives a more enjoyable impression than hiragana or kanji.

Review the katakana words in the picture.

[Exercise 1] Match the katakana to the correct pronunciation.

セール　・　　　　　・　fe a

オープン　・　　　　　・　ō pu n

キャンペーン　・　　　・　sē ru

フェア　・　　　　　・　kya n pē n

ブランド　・　　　　　・　bu ra n do

[Exercise 2] Practice writing the characters in the boxes provided.

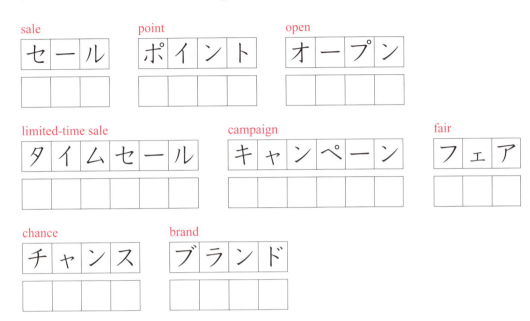

[Exercise 3] Translate the English words into katakana.

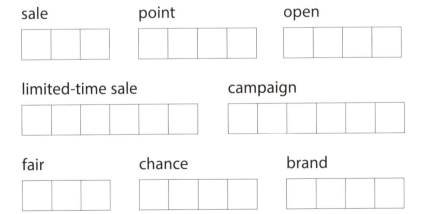

Lesson 24

Instruments 楽器(がっき)

Just as with sports, traditional Japanese instruments (*taiko*, *koto*, *shakuhachi*, etc.) have their own kanji, while katakana is used for instruments which were introduced to Japan from abroad.

Review the katakana words in the picture.

[Exercise 1] Match the katakana to the correct pronunciation.

ピアノ　・　　　　　・　do ra mu

ギター　・　　　　　・　gi tā

ドラム　・　　　　　・　pi a no

サックス　・　　　　・　sa kku su

バンド　・　　　　　・　ba n do

[Exercise 2] Practice writing the characters in the boxes provided.

piano
ピ	ア	ノ

guitar
ギ	タ	ー

drum
ド	ラ	ム

bass
ベ	ー	ス

trombone
ト	ロ	ン	ボ	ー	ン

trumpet
ト	ラ	ン	ペ	ッ	ト

saxophone
サ	ッ	ク	ス

band
バ	ン	ド

[Exercise 3] Translate the English words into katakana.

piano

guitar

drum

bass

trombone

trumpet

saxophone

band

Chapter 4

People, Places, and Business

第4章　人・場所・ビジネスに関するカタカナ

Lesson 25

Countries 国名(こくめい)

Though a few country names like イギリス and ドイツ have pronunciations that differ significantly from English, many of them will be quite recognizable when spoken. But because Japanese syllables are relatively unstressed, long words such as オーストラリア and ウズベキスタン can be tricky for foreigners to pronounce.

アイスランド a i su ra n do *Iceland*	ウズベキスタン u zu be ki su ta n *Uzbekistan*	ケニア ke ni a *Kenya*
アフガニスタン a fu ga ni su ta n *Afghanistan*	エジプト e ji pu to *Egypt*	コロンビア ko ro n bi a *Colombia*
アメリカ a me ri ka *United States*	エチオピア e chi o pi a *Ethiopia*	サウジアラビア sa u ji a ra bi a *Saudi Arabia*
アルゼンチン a ru ze n chi n *Argentina*	オーストラリア ō su to ra ri a *Australia*	シリア shi ri a *Syria*
イギリス i gi ri su *England*	オーストリア ō su to ri a *Austria*	シンガポール shi n ga pō ru *Singapore*
イタリア i ta ri a *Italy*	オランダ o ra n da *Holland / Netherlands*	スーダン sū da n *Sudan*
インド i n do *India*	ガーナ gā na *Ghana*	スイス su i su *Switzerland*
インドネシア in do ne shi a *Indonesia*	カナダ ka na da *Canada*	スウェーデン su wē de n *Sweden*
イラン i ra n *Iran*	キューバ kyū ba *Cuba*	スペイン su pe i n *Spain*
ウガンダ u ga n da *Uganda*	ギリシャ gi ri sha *Greece*	スリランカ su ri ra n ka *Sri Lanka*
ウクライナ u ku ra i na *Ukraine*	クウェート ku wē to *Kuwait*	ソマリア so ma ri a *Somalia*

タイ ta i *Thailand*	フィジー fi jī *Fiji*	ベルギー be ru gī *Belgium*
チリ chi ri *Chile*	フィリピン fi ri pi n *Philippines*	ポーランド pō ra n do *Poland*
デンマーク de n mā ku *Denmark*	フィンランド fi n ra n do *Finland*	マダガスカル ma da ga su ka ru *Madagascar*
ドイツ do i tsu *Germany*	プエルトリコ pu e ru to ri ko *Puerto Rico*	メキシコ me ki shi ko *Mexico*
トルコ to ru ko *Turkey*	ブラジル bu ra ji ru *Brazil*	モロッコ mo ro kko *Morocco*
ニュージーランド nyū jī ra n do *New Zealand*	フランス fu ra n su *France*	ルワンダ ru wa n da *Rwanda*
ノルウェー no ru wē *Norway*	ベトナム be to na mu *Vietnam*	ロシア ro shi a *Russia*
パラオ pa ra o *Palau*	ペルー pe rū *Peru*	

Lesson 26

English Names 英語名(えいごめい)

Japanese has a small number of unique syllables, which can make it difficult to accurately express your own name in katakana. It is a good idea to practice until you can read and write your own name quickly, however.

アレキサンダー a re ki san dā *Alexander*	ケイト ke i to *Kate*
アン a n *Ann*	サリー sa rī *Sally*
アンディ a n di *Andy*	スーザン sū za n *Susan*
イアン i a n *Ian*	ソフィア so fi a *Sophia*
エイドリアン e i do ri an *Adrian*	トム to mu *Tom*
エリック e ri kku *Eric*	ジェシー je shī *Jesse*
オリヴィア o ri bi a *Olivia*	ジョーン jō n *Joan*
クリス ku ri su *Chris*	ジョン jo n *John*
クリスティーヌ ku ri su tī nu *Christina*	タイラー ta i rā *Tyler*

ナタリー na ta rī *Natalie*	モニカ mo ni ka *Monica*
ビリー bi rī *Billy*	ライアン ra i a n *Ryan*
ヘンリー he n rī *Henry*	ルーク rū ku *Luke*
マイク ma i ku *Mike*	レベッカ re be kka *Rebecca*
マルタ ma ru ta *Marta*	ロバート ro bā to *Robert*
ミッシェル mi sshe ru *Michelle*	ワイアット wa i a tto *Wyatt*

Lesson 27

Companies 会社名
<small>かいしゃめい</small>

Katakana is not just used for the names of foreign companies. Japanese companies often use it often as well because it has a more obvious pronunciation than kanji and works well as a company logo.

アウディ a u di *Audi*	キヤノン kya no n *Canon*
アサヒ a sa hi *Asahi*	キリン ki ri n *Kirin*
アップル a ppu ru *Apple*	グーグル gū gu ru *Google*
アマゾン a ma zo n *Amazon*	グッチ gu tchi *Gucci*
イケア i ke a *Ikea*	ケロッグ ke ro ggu *Kellogg*
インテル i n te ru *Intel*	サムスン sa mu su n *Samsung*
エルメス e ru me su *Hermes*	サントリー sa n to rī *Suntory*
オラクル o ra ku ru *Oracle*	シャープ shā pu *Sharp*

スズキ su zu ki *Suzuki*	ボーイング bō i n gu *Boeing*
ソフトバンク so fu to ba n ku *SoftBank*	ホンダ ho n da *Honda*
トヨタ to yo ta *Toyota*	マツダ ma tsu da *Mazda*
ネスレ ne su re *Nestle*	ヤマハ ya ma ha *Yamaha*
パナソニック pa na so ni kku *Panasonic*	ユニクロ yu ni ku ro *Uniqlo*
フォード fo do *Ford*	ルイ・ヴィトン ru i bi to n *Louis Vuitton*
フォルクスワーゲン fo ru ku su wā ge n *Volkswagen*	

V is written as ヴ but pronounced with a [b] sound.

Lesson 28

Business Terms ビジネス用語(bi ji ne su yō go)

Due to the effects of globalization, katakana is now often used to express English words. But true English pronunciations can sometimes be difficult for Japanese people to understand, so if you use them try to speak in a slow, even tone.

アジェンダ a je n da *agenda*	キャンセル kya n se ru *cancel*
アポ a po *appointment*	クライアント ku ra i a n to *client*
アライアンス a ra i a n su *alliance*	クラウド ku ra u do *cloud*
イニシアチブ i ni shi a chi bu *initiative*	コンセプト ko n se pu to *concept*
イノベーション i no bē sho n *innovation*	コンセンサス ko n se n sa su *consensus*
インターフェース i n tā fē su *interface*	コンピテンシー ko n pi te n shī *competency*
ウィンウィン wi n wi n *win-win*	シナジー shi na jī *synergy*
キャパ kya pa *capacity*	スキーム su kī mu *scheme*

スケジュール su ke jū ru *schedule*	プロジェクト pu ro je ku to *project*
タイト ta i to *tight*	マイルストーン ma i ru su tō n *milestone*
タスク ta su ku *task*	ミーティング mī ti n gu *meeting*
フェーズ fē zu *phase*	モデリング mo de ri n gu *modeling*
ブラッシュアップ bu ra sshu a ppu *brush up*	ワークショップ wā ku sho ppu *workshop*

Katakana words borrowed from English are heavily used in Japanese business.

Lesson 29

Computer Terms コンピューター用語
_{ko n pyū tā よう ご}

Virtually all terms related to computers are loanwords and thus written in katakana, but be careful with some of the incongruous pronunciations like アプリ and ルーター.

アイコン	サーバー
a i ko n	sā bā
icon	*server*

アカウント	スペック
a ka u n to	su pe kku
account	*spec(ification)*

アプリ	ダウンロード
a pu ri	da u n rō do
app	*download*

インストール	タスクバー
i n su tō ru	ta su ku bā
install	*taskbar*

ウイルス	チャット
u i ru su	cha tto
virus	*chat*

オフライン	ドメイン
o fu ra i n	do me i n
offline	*domain*

オンライン	ハッカー
o n ra i n	ha kkā
online	*hacker*

カーソル	バナー
kā so ru	ba nā
cursor	*banner*

ファイル fa i ru *file*	モデム mo de mu *modem*
ブックマーク bu kku mā ku *bookmark*	ユーザーネーム yū zā nē mu *username*
ブラウザ bu ra u za *browser*	ライブラリ ra i bu ra ri *library*
プロバイダ pu ro ba i da *provider*	リンク ri n ku *link*
ポインター po i n tā *pointer*	ルーター rū tā *router*
マウス ma u su *mouse*	レス re su *response*
メール mē ru *email*	

Chapter 5

Wasei-Eigo and Other Terms

第5章　和製英語など

Lesson 30

Wasei-Eigo 1 和製英語 1

These are words that Japanese people created based on English words. Some of the most commonly used phrases are provided here, but many others exist.

アットホーム　*cozy, at-home feeling*
a tto hō mu

[例]　うちの職場は、アットホームです。
Uchi no shokuba wa, atto hōmu desu.

[Ex.]　*Our office atmosphere is cozy.*

アラサー　*around thirty years old*

[例]　アラサーだから結婚を考えないと…。

[Ex.]　*I'm around thirty years old…it's time to think about marriage.*

アメリカンドッグ　*corn dog*
a me ri ka n do ggu

インロック　*lock one's keys inside (a car)*
i n ro kku

イメチェン　*change one's appearance*
i me che n

[例]　イメチェンしたい。
Imechen shitai.

[Ex.]　*I want to change my appearance.*

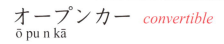

オープンカー　*convertible*
ō pu n kā

オーダーメイド　*custom(-made)*
ō dā me i do

カンニング　*cheating (on a test)*
ka n ni n gu

ガードマン　*security guard*
gā do ma n

キーホルダー　*key chain*
kī ho ru dā

84

キャッチボール　playing catch (with a ball)
kya tchi bō ru

- 例　友達とキャッチボールする。
  Tomodachi to kyatchi bōru suru.
- Ex.　I'm going to play catch with my friend.
- 例　田中さんは、会話のキャッチボールができない。
  Tanaka-san wa, kaiwa no kyatchi bōru ga dekinai.
- Ex.　Mr. Tanaka is not good at keeping a conversation going.

クレーム　complaint
ku rē mu

- 例　店で品物にクレームをつけた。
  Mise de shinamono ni kurēmu o tsuketa.
- Ex.　I complained about an item at the store.

クラクション　car horn
ku ra ku sho n

- 例　車のクラクションがうるさい。
  Kuruma no kurakushon ga urusai.
- Ex.　The car horn is loud.

コンセント　electrical outlet/socket
ko n se n to

コストダウン　reduce costs
ko su to da u n

- 例　うちの会社はコストダウンが必要ですね。
  Uchi no kaisha wa kosutodaun ga hitsuyō desu ne.
- Ex.　Our company needs to reduce costs.

コピーバンド　cover band
ko pī ba n do

サラリーマン　salaried employee
sa ra rī ma n

セロテープ　cellophane tape
se ro tē pu

シール　sticker
shī ru

スマート　slim
su mā to

- 例　やせてスマートになった！
  Yasete sumāto ni natta!
- Ex.　I lost some weight and look slimmer now.

Lesson 31

Wasei-Eigo 2　和製英語 2

Here are some more *wasei-eigo* terms. An English native might hesitate to use them since they sound so strange, but doing so will make your speech sound very natural to a native Japanese speaker.

タレント　*T.V. personality*
ta re n to

チャームポイント　*one's attractive qualities*
chā mu po i n to

例　君のチャームポイントは目だね。
　　Kimi no chāmupointo wa me da ne.

Ex.　Your eyes are most attractive quality.

ドンマイ　*don't worry (said for encouragement)*
do n ma i

例　A：あ〜あ　テストだめだった〜。
　　A : Ā~ tesuto dame datta~.
　　B：ドンマイ　ドンマイ、次があるよ。
　　B : Donmai donmai, tsugi ga aru yo.

Ex.　Oh no... I failed my test.
　　Don't worry about it. Tomorrow is another day.

ナイーブ　*sensitive*　　　　バイキング　*buffet*
na ī bu　　　　　　　　　　ba i ki n gu

ハイテンション　*excited*
ha i te n sho n

例　今日はハイテンションだね。
　　Kyō wa haitenshon da ne.

Ex.　You seem excited today.

ハンドルキーパー　*designated driver*
ha n do ru kī pā

フリーダイヤル　*toll-free*　　　　フリーサイズ　*one size fits all*
fu rī da i ya ru　　　　　　　　　fu rī sa i zu

ファイト　*Go for it!*
fa i to

例　がんばっていこう！ファイト！
　　Ganbatte ikou! faito!

Ex.　Let's give 'em our best! Go!

ヘビロテ   heavy rotation (such as a song on a radio station)
he bi ro te

ペットボトル   plastic bottle
pe tto bo to ru

ペアルック   matching outfits
pe a ru kku

ペーパードライバー   someone who has a driver's license but never drives anywhere
pē pā do ra i bā

ベッドタウン   commuter town
be ddo ta u n

ホッチキス   stapler
ho tchi ki su

マイバッグ   one's own shopping bag
ma i ba ggu

マイペース   at one's own pace / not easily influenced
ma i pē su

例　田中さんはマイペースですね。
　　Tanaka-san wa maipēsu desu ne.

Ex.　Mr. Tanaka is always in his own little world.

マイホーム   self-owned home (not rented)
ma i hō mu

マンツーマン   one-on-one (lesson)
ma n tsū ma n

例　レッスンをマンツーマンで受ける。
　　Ressun o mantsūman de ukeru.

Ex.　I take one-on-one lessons.

ラブラブ   very affectionate or romantic
ra bu ra bu

例　あの夫婦はいつもラブラブだね。
　　Ano fūfu wa itsumo raburabu da ne.

Ex.　That married couple is always very affectionate.

ユーフォー   U.F.O.
yū fō

ワンパターン   monotonous
wa n pa tān

例　仕事が毎日ワンパターンでつまらない。
　　Shigoto ga mainichi wanpatān de tsumaranai.

Ex.　My day-to-day work is monotonous and boring.

Lesson 32

Other Terms　その他(た)

Although kanji do exist for some of these words, they are often written in katakana for a variety of reasons; their kanji might be difficult, for instance, or the writer just wanted to make use of katakana's visual appeal.

Words have difficult kanji

オレ　*I (casual expression used by men)*
o re

ヒザ　*knee*　　　ワキ　*armpit*　　　ケガ　*injury*
hi za　　　　　wa ki　　　　　　ke ga

バラ　*rose*　　　カビ　*mold*
ba ra　　　　　ka bi

Slang

マジ？　*Are you serious?*　　ヤバイ　*dangerous*
ma ji　　　　　　　　　　　ya ba i

ネタバレ　*spoiler*　　　　　モヤモヤ　*fuzzy / feel gloomy*
ne ta ba re　　　　　　　　mo ya mo ya

Animals / Plants

ブタ　*pig*　　　　　　　　ヤギ　*goat*
bu ta　　　　　　　　　　ya gi

アサガオ　*morning glory*　　ヒマワリ　*sunflower*
a sa ga o　　　　　　　　　hi ma wa ri

Visual effects

1. To lessen a word's impact

ジャマ　*disturb*　　　　　　ダメ　*not allowed*
ja ma　　　　　　　　　　　da me

ワガママ　*selfish*　　　　　ケンカ　*fight / quarrel*
wa ga ma ma　　　　　　　　ke n ka

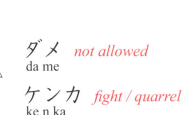

2. To make a word look cooler

オシャレ *fashionable*
o sha re

カッコイイ *cool*
ka kko i i

3. To express a sound

ドーン *low thump or boom*
dō n

トントン *knocking or drumming sound*
to n to n

ザーザー *sound of heavy rainfall*
zā zā

ゴシゴシ *scrubbing sound*
go shi go shi

4. To express an animal sound

ワンワン *dog*
wa n wa n

ニャーニャー *cat*
nyā nyā

ブーブー *pig*
bū bū

モー *cow*
mō

5. To express a scream

キャー *(woman)*
kyā

ワー *(man)*
wā

ウォー *(monster)*
wō

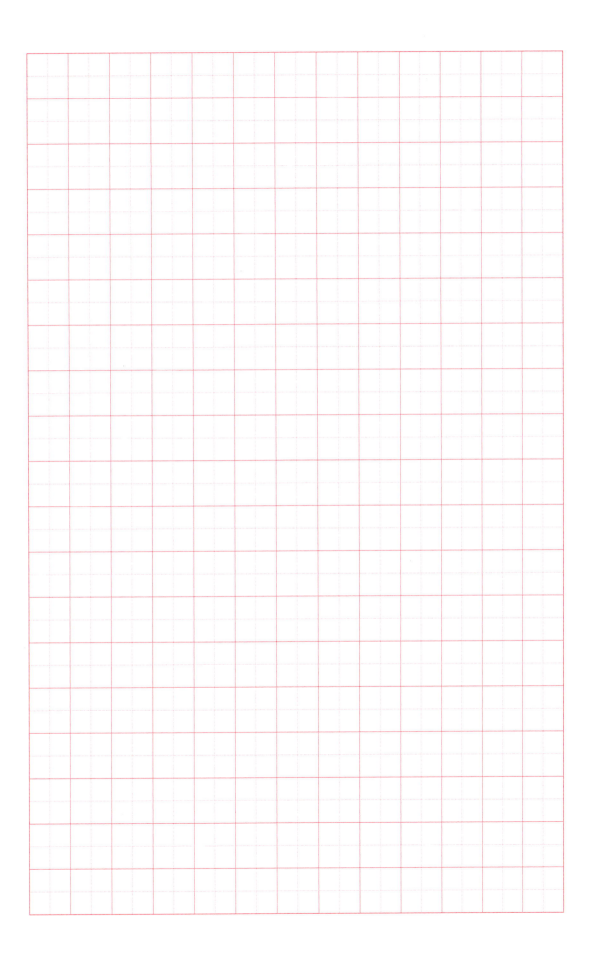

EASY AND FUN
KATAKANA

2017年　4月5日　第1刷発行
2024年　9月6日　第3刷発行

著　者　小川　清美
発行者　賀川　洋
発行所　IBCパブリッシング株式会社
　　　　〒162-0804　東京都新宿区中里町29番3号　菱秀神楽坂ビル
　　　　Tel. 03-3513-4511　Fax. 03-3513-4512
　　　　www.ibcpub.co.jp
印刷所　中央精版印刷株式会社

© 小川清美2017

Printed in Japan

落丁本・乱丁本は、小社宛にお送りください。送料小社負担にてお取り替えいたします。
本書の無断複写（コピー）は著作権法上での例外を除き禁じられています。

ISBN978-4-7946-0473-6